FACT FINDERS

All kinds of homes

John Foster

Oxford University Press

Oxford University Press, Great Clarendon Street, Oxford OX2 6DP

Oxford   New York
Athens   Auckland   Bangkok   Bogota   Buenos Aires   Calcutta   Cape Town   Chennai
Dar es Salaam   Delhi   Florence   Hong Kong   Istanbul   Karachi   Kuala Lumpur
Madrid   Melbourne   Mexico City   Mumbai   Nairobi   Paris   São Paulo   Singapore
Taipei   Tokyo   Toronto   Warsaw

and associated companies in
Berlin   Ibadan

Oxford is a trade mark of Oxford University Press

© Oxford University Press
First published by Oxford University Press 1994
Reprinted 1995, 1998

ISBN 0 19 916644 7
Available in packs
Houses and homes pack (one of each title)   ISBN 0 19 916650 1
Houses and homes class pack (six of each title)   ISBN 0 19 916651 X

Teacher's Guide ISBN 0 19 916670 6

A CIP catalogue record for this book is available from the British Library.

Acknowledgements

The Publisher would like to thank the following for permission to reproduce
photographs: Arcaid (7, 12, 18 [right]), English Heritage (21), Habinteg Housing
Association Ltd (13 [both]), Jane and Rupert Hannen (23 [both]), Images (cover,
16, 22), The National Trust (20), Topham Picture Source (18 [left])

Illustrated by Tony Ansell (4, 5) and Mel Wright (9)

Printed and bound in Hong Kong

Contents

Page

▶ All kinds of homes 4

▶ Terraced houses 6

▶ Semi-detached houses 8

▶ Detached houses 10

▶ Bungalows 12

▶ Flats 14

▶ Houses in the country 16

▶ Homes that can move 18

▶ Houses to visit 20

▶ Old buildings, new homes 22

▶ Index 24

All kinds of homes

The family are looking for a new home.

Your home is the place where you live.

There are many different kinds of houses
and homes.
This book tells you about some of them.

Terraced houses

These houses are all joined together.

They are in a row.

The row of houses is called a terrace.

Each house is called a terraced house.

These houses are also terraced houses.

They were built a long time ago.

Semi-detached houses

These houses are built in pairs.

Each house is joined to one other house.

They are called semi-detached houses.

The two houses have a wall between them.
The rooms in each house are the same size,
but they may look different.

Detached houses

This house is not joined to another house.
It is called a detached house.
Some detached houses have
gardens all round them.

This detached house has two levels.

Each level is called a storey.

The house has space for a garage.

Bungalows

This house has only one storey.

It has no stairs.

It is called a bungalow.

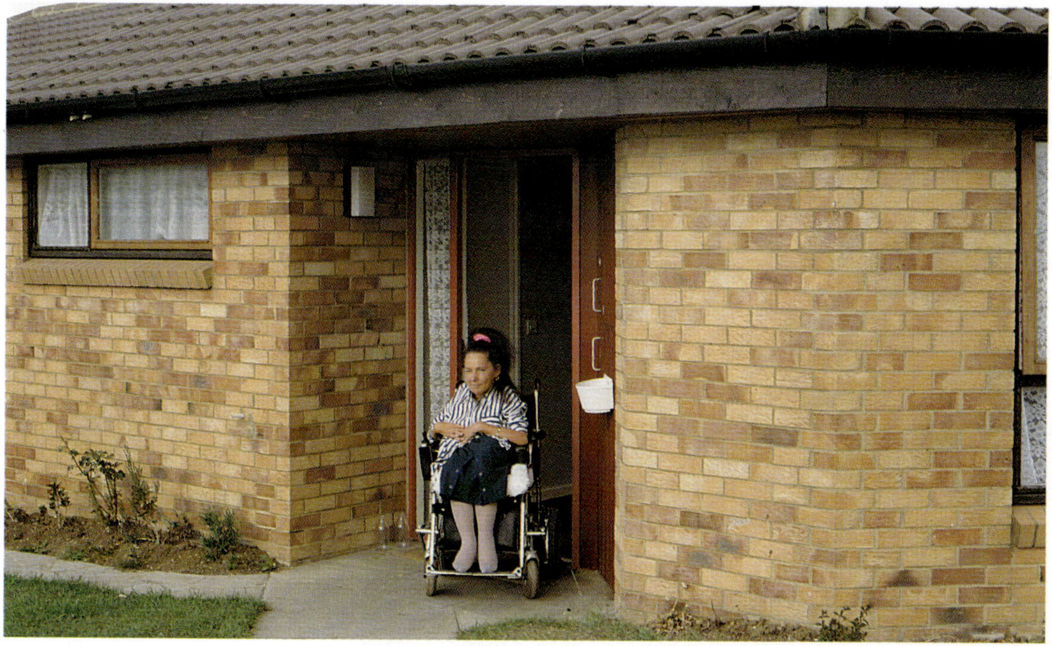

These disabled people live in
special bungalows.
There is room for wheelchairs, and
the people can reach things easily.

Flats

There are many homes in this building.

Each home is called a flat.

Many different buildings have

flats in them.

▲ Lifts

Tall blocks of flats are called
tower blocks.
They need lifts to take people up
to their flats.

Houses in the country

This house is on a farm.

It is called a farmhouse.

Farmhouses can be old or new.

These houses are in a village.

Some village houses are called cottages.

Some old cottages have thatched roofs.

Homes that can move

Some people live in caravans.

Others live on houseboats.

These people sometimes move their homes

to different places.

Some people live in bigger caravans.
Caravans like these are often called
mobile homes.

Houses to visit

Some houses are very large, and
have lots of rooms.
These houses are sometimes called
stately homes.

Sometimes, the owners live in part

of the stately home.

People pay to visit the rest of the home.

This stately home has a café for visitors.

Old buildings, new homes

Some people buy old buildings and
change them into homes.
Once, this building was a windmill.
Now, it is someone's home.

Once, this building was a school.

Now, it is someone's home.

Index

bungalow   12–13

caravan   18–19

cottage   17

detached house   10–11

farmhouse   16

flat   14–15

houseboat   18

mobile home   19

old building   22–23

semi-detached house   8–9

stately home   20–21

terraced house   6–7

tower block   15